teach me about

Relatives

Childrens Press
School and Library Edition
Published 1987

Copyright © 1986 by Joy Berry
Living Skills Press, Sebastopol, CA
All rights reserved.
Printed in the United States of America

No part of this book may be reproduced by any mechanical,
photographic or electronic process, or in the form of a
phonographic recording, nor may it be stored in a retrieval
system, transmitted, or otherwise be copied for public or
private use without written permission of the publisher.

Managing Editor: Ellen Klarberg
Copy Editor: Kate Dickey
Contributing Writer: Kathleen McBride
Contributing Editors: Libby Byers, Maureen Dryden, Yona Flemming
Editorial Assistant: Sandy Passarino

Art Director: Laurie Westdahl
Design and Production: Abigail Johnston
Illustrator: Bartholomew
Inker: Susie Hornig
Production Assistant: Lillian Cram
Composition: Curt Chelin

teach me about

Relatives

By JOY BERRY

Illustrated by Bartholomew

 CHILDRENS PRESS ®

CHICAGO

The people who are a part of
your family are called
your relatives.

You are my daddy and mommy.

Yes, and we are also your relatives.

Your daddy has a mother.

Your daddy's mother is

your grandmother.

7

Your daddy has a father.

Your daddy's father is

your grandfather.

9

Your mommy has a mother.

Your mommy's mother is

your grandmother.

Your mommy has a father.

Your mommy's father is

your grandfather.

Some daddies have sisters.

Maybe your daddy has a

sister. If he does,

your daddy's sister

is your aunt.

15

Some daddies have brothers.

Maybe your daddy has a

brother. If he does,

your daddy's brother

is your uncle.

Some mommies have sisters.

Maybe your mommy has a

sister. If she does,

your mommy's sister

is your aunt.

Some mommies have brothers.

Maybe your mommy has a

brother. If she does,

your mommy's brother

is your uncle.

Some uncles are married.

Maybe your uncle is married.

If he is married,

your uncle's wife

is your aunt.

Some aunts are married.

Maybe your aunt is married.

If she is married,

your aunt's husband

is your uncle.

Some aunts and uncles

have children.

Maybe your aunts and uncles

have children. If they do,

your aunts' and uncles'

children are your cousins.

Your parents, grandparents,

aunts, uncles, and cousins

are a part of your family.

They are your relatives.

Relatives are people

you can love.

You can let your relatives know

you love them.

You can be kind to them.

You can say nice things to them.

They like to hear words like

- please

- may I

- thank you

- excuse me

- I love you

31

You can be a nice person

around your relatives.

Try not to be selfish.

Try not to be rude.

33

You can do nice things

for your relatives.

Cooperate with them when

they are taking care of you.

Help them in any way

that you can.